"In his first book, author George Smith combines geography and messages about acceptance and caring in a book aimed at young readers. ...The book is filled with ups & downs that keep young readers turning the page, while offering adults the opportunities to teach or reinforce a lesson or two."

Renee Kiriluk Hill
Hunterdon Observer

"This summer ... saw the release of a new book that promises to resonate with youngsters from the Midcoast area."

Lincoln Country Weekly

Access Online Resources

Visit the URL and place the book access code.

http://www.lumoslearning.com/a/tedbooks

Book Access Code: CRSRB-48612-P

Curious Reader Series: The Journey of the Little Red Boat

Author	-	George Smith
Contributing Author	-	Harini N.
Illustrator	-	Susan Pribish
Executive Producer	-	Mukunda Krishnaswamy
Designer	-	Sowmya R.

COPYRIGHT ©2018 by Lumos Information Services, LLC. **ALL RIGHTS RESERVED.** No part of this work covered by the copyright hereon may be reproduced or used in any form or by any means graphic, electronic, or mechanical, including photocopying, recording, taping, Web distribution or information storage and retrieval systems- without the written permission of the publisher.

ISBN-10: 1-949855-00-7

ISBN-13: 978-1-949855-00-5

Printed in the United States of America

For permissions and additional information contact:

Lumos Information Services, LLC
Email: support@lumoslearning.com
PO Box 1575, Piscataway,
NJ 08855-1575

Tel: (732) 384-0146
Fax: (866) 283-6471
http://www.LumosLearning.com

About the Author:

George Smith, a children's book author and publisher, has been conducting writing workshops at schools since 2004. He is passionate about helping young writers turn their creative story ideas to captivating stories that others would enjoy reading. He has authored two children's books, a marine life guide book for science teachers and functioned as an editor for several publications. He lives in Lakewood, New Jersey and loves to travel.

Table of Content

Introduction	1
Story: The Journey of the Little Red Boat	2
Listen to this story on StepUp App	52
Readability and Related Details	52
Exercises	53
Answer Key and Detailed Explanation	55
How Author's Develop Story Ideas	56
Instructional Information	60

Introduction

One of the most enriching experiences for a child is to enjoy stories. Lumos Learning has launched the Curious Reader Series to help children become successful readers. This book series is the perfect package to get students interested and engaged in reading. Each book in the series is designed for a specific reading-level and includes activities that improve both reading and writing skills. Students will have the opportunity to listen to the story online and answer questions to get immediate feedback.

This series includes fictions by expert authors along with tips and pointers to help children write on their own. The stories and articles combine facts with new ideas to make reading more enjoyable for children.

About The Little Red Boat

The Story of the Little Red Boat is an exciting tale for children in grades K-3. This book is a part of Lumos Curious Reader series and is designed to help young readers enjoy the story as well as develop their critical reading skills. It includes exercises to create opportunities for young readers to identify settings, plots, characters, etc. The exercises are designed to help them recognize how the author has developed the story. This tedBook also includes access to engaging and interactive online resources.

The Journey of the Little Red Boat

MAP

Once upon a time there was a little red boat that lived on a river, near the coast of Maine.

The little red boat was happy.

She belonged to a very nice family, who kept her tied to their dock.

Draw and Color

Notes

From the dock,
she could watch everything
that was happening on the river.

There were lobster boats
with lobstermen hauling their lobster traps,
motorboats full of people going for a boat ride,
and sailboats being pushed by the wind.

Draw and Color

Notes

Sometimes, the family that owned the little red boat
climbed into her and rowed out to their sailboat.
They tied her behind the sailboat,
and as they sailed,
the little red boat followed.

The little red boat liked to go sailing,
because she could see other parts of the river,
far from her dock.

The sailboat and the little red boat were good friends.

Draw and Color

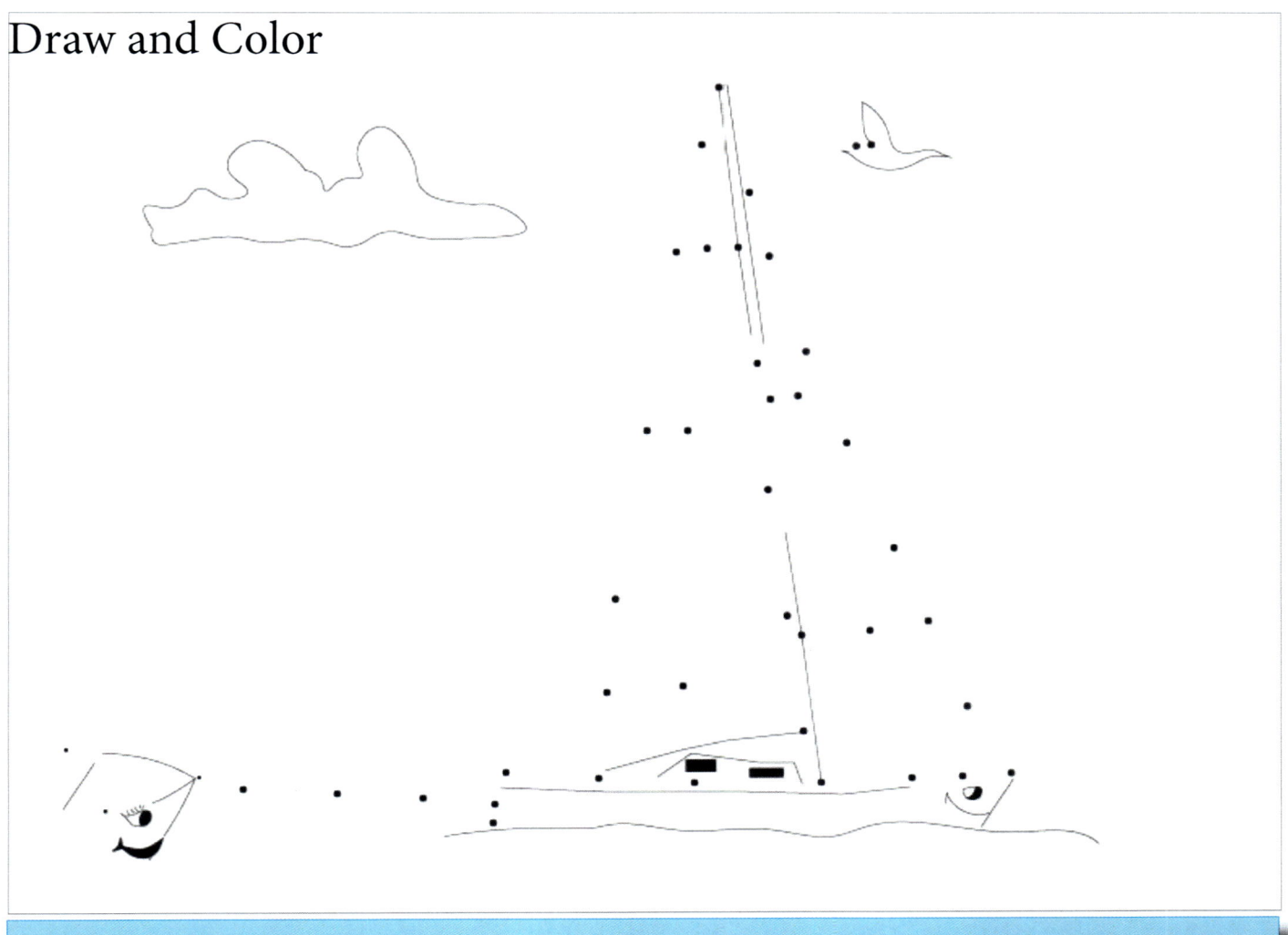

Notes

After many years,
the family sold the sailboat,
and the new owners took it away.

But the new owners did not take the little red boat.
They already had a boat of their own.
The family did not need the little red boat,
so they left her tied to the dock, day after day.

No one came to visit her. She felt sad, lonely,
unwanted, and not important at all.

Draw and Color

Notes

One summer, the rain poured down
and the winds blew for several days.
The little red boat filled with water, almost to the top of her seats.
She became so heavy that the rope that tied her to the dock
could not hold her anymore — and it broke.

Then the wind blew the little red boat away from the dock.
The tide[1] was going out toward the ocean,
and helped the wind push the little red boat
down the river, away from her home.

---

[1] tide: The rise and fall of water in an ocean and in the rivers and streams that flow into the ocean, that occurs about once every 12 hours. The tide causes a current that will move a boat floating in the water.

Draw and Color

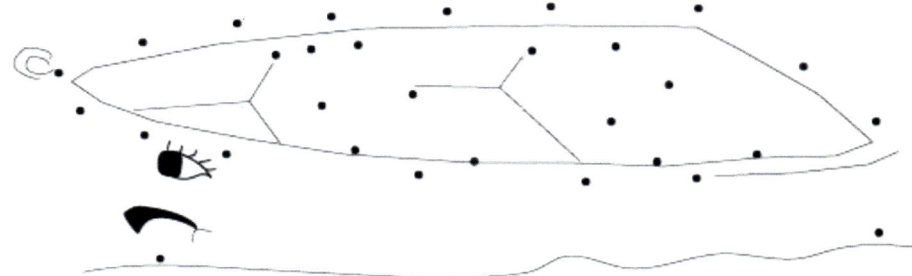

Notes

The little red boat was afraid.
She had never been out on the river alone.

She had always been safely attached to the sailboat,
and the sailboat, and the family,
made sure that the little red boat was safe.

But this time, she was alone,
and there was no one to protect her.
Although the rain had stopped,
it was cloudy and cold, and there was no sun.

Draw and Color

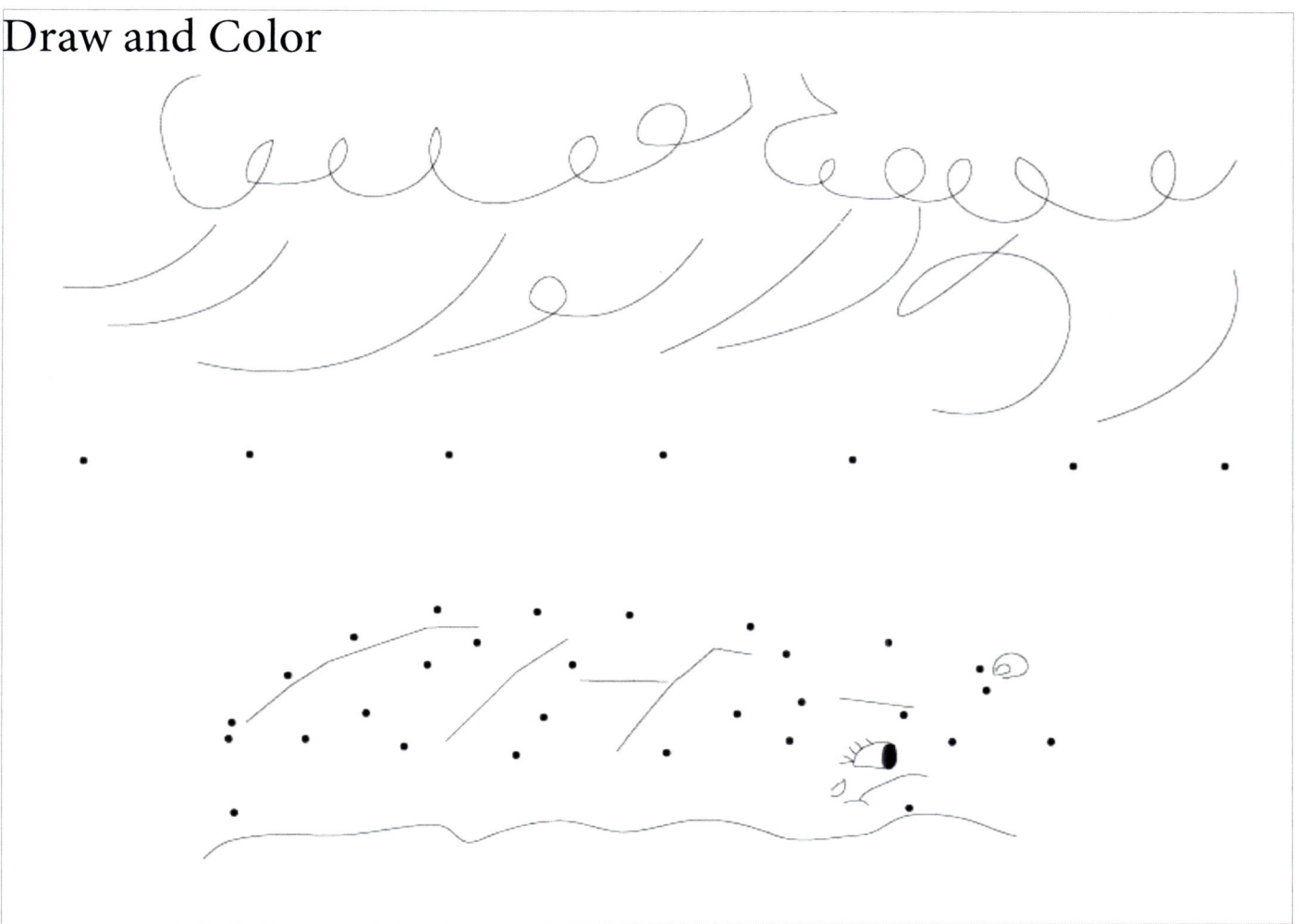

Notes

Ouch!!
Suddenly, the little red boat felt a hard bump on her side,
as the wind blew her onto a rock.

"Help, help!!" said the little red boat.
But the rock said, "Go away,
stop bumping me, you are too heavy!!"

And the wind and tide[1]
blew the little red boat away from the rock.

Draw and Color

Notes

As the little red boat drifted down the river,
she came to a place
where several sailboats were anchored.

The sailboats were white and shiny, and very pretty.
The little red boat was happy when she saw the sailboats.
Surely they would let her stay there and sleep,
and protect her until her family found her.

But as the little red boat drifted toward the sailboats,
they shouted, "Go away!!
You are going to bump us and scratch our paint!! Go away."
The little red boat was very sad.
The wind blew harder, and the little red boat drifted
further down the river — scared, sad and alone.

Draw and Color

Notes

As the little red boat floated down the river, she saw a rock. Sitting on the rock was a seal.

The little red boat said,
"I am alone and afraid.
Please Mr. Seal, swim with me and keep me company.
In a few hours it will be dark and I will not be able to see at all."

But the seal said, "I cannot stay with you.
I am hungry and I must find some fish to eat. Sorry."
And he swam away.

Draw and Color

Notes

Some black sea birds, called cormorants,
were standing on another rock in the river.

As the little red boat drifted toward them,
she became more and more excited.

Surely they would let her stay with them until morning,
so she would have someone to talk to.

But, it was dark, and the black sea birds
thought the little red boat was a monster.
They squawked to each other to fly away.
"But I am a lost boat, not a monster," cried the little red boat.

But it was too late. The cormorants had flown away.

Draw and Color

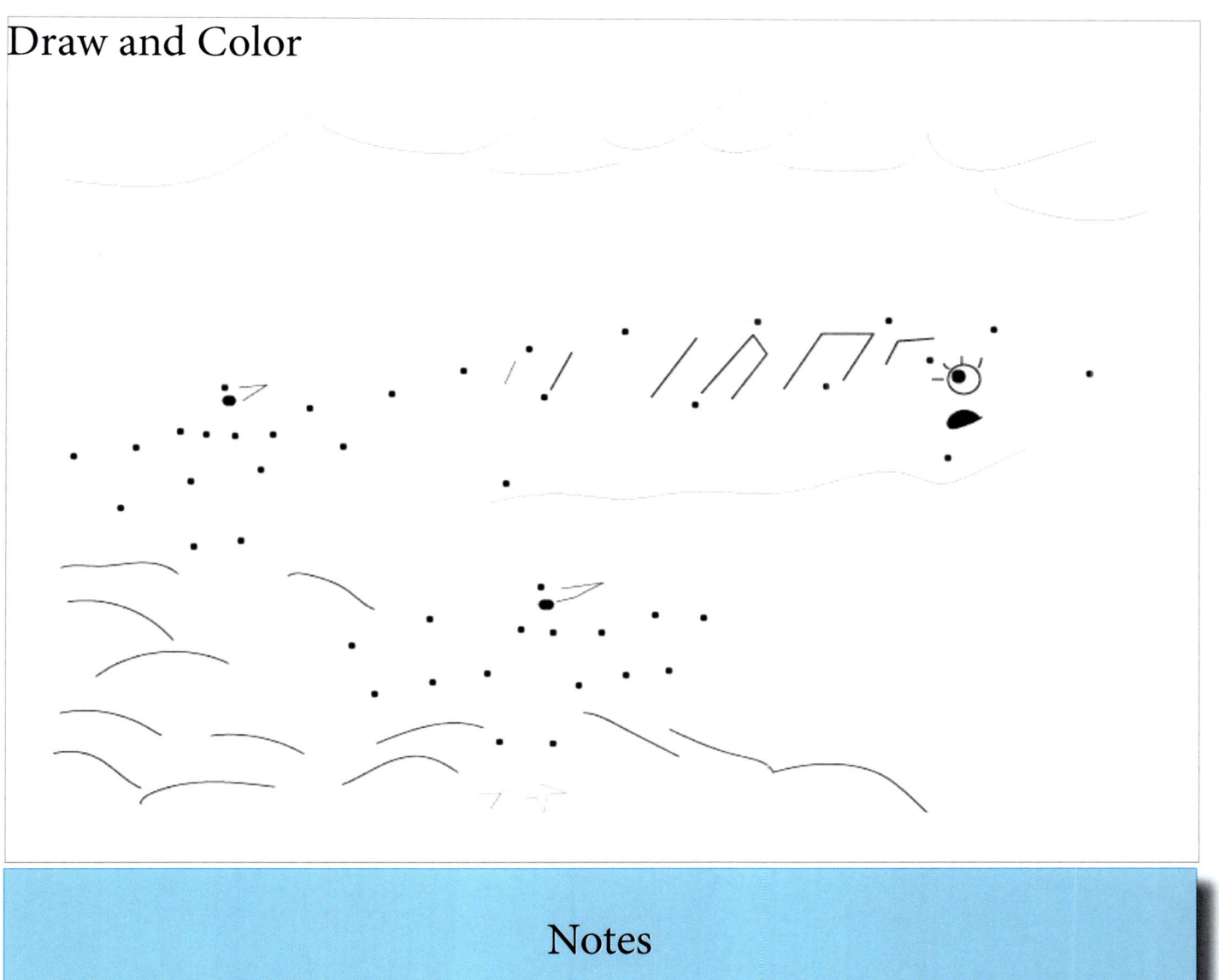

Notes

After all this, the little red boat became very sad and started to cry.
She said to herself, "The wind and the tide[1]
will push me down the river and into the ocean.
The big waves will come over my sides and fill me with water.
I will sink to the bottom and no one will ever find me."
She cried and cried. Finally she was so tired, she fell asleep.

But the little red boat was lucky. She drifted to a cove
between an island and the shore that was
sheltered from the wind and the tide[1].
The wind stopped blowing, and the water became calm,
and the little red boat was safe now.
She slept all night, until the sun came up in the morning.

---

[1]tide: The rise and fall of water in an ocean and in the rivers and streams that flow into the ocean, that occurs about once every 12 hours. The tide causes a current that will move a boat floating in the water.

Draw and Color

Notes

On the shore of the cove was a pretty white house, with a long green front lawn.

A grandpa and grandma lived in the house. In the summer, their granddaughter, Grace came from Massachusetts to stay with them until school started in the fall.

Grace loved to visit grandma and grandpa.

Draw and Color

Notes

They played games at the kitchen table and on the front lawn.

Grace loved to walk down the lawn to the cove,
sit on the dock and dangle her feet in the cool water.

She loved to climb over the rocks, looking for little crabs and fish
trapped in pools of water — left there as the tide went out.

She wished grandpa had a boat so they could go fishing,
or row across the cove to the island to pick flowers.

But he didn't have one, so Grace stayed on the shore.

Draw and Color

Notes

One morning Grace woke up early, and tiptoed quietly to the kitchen.
Shhh!! — grandpa and grandma were still asleep.

When Grace reached the kitchen, she did what she always did first —
looked out the window at the long green lawn and the cove.

But this morning, there was a surprise waiting for her.
In the cove something red was floating.
Can you see it? Can you guess what it is?

Grace thought it looked like a boat,
but she wasn't sure — it was far away.
She ran down the lawn for a better look, and yes, it was a boat!!

It was a little red boat.

Draw and Color

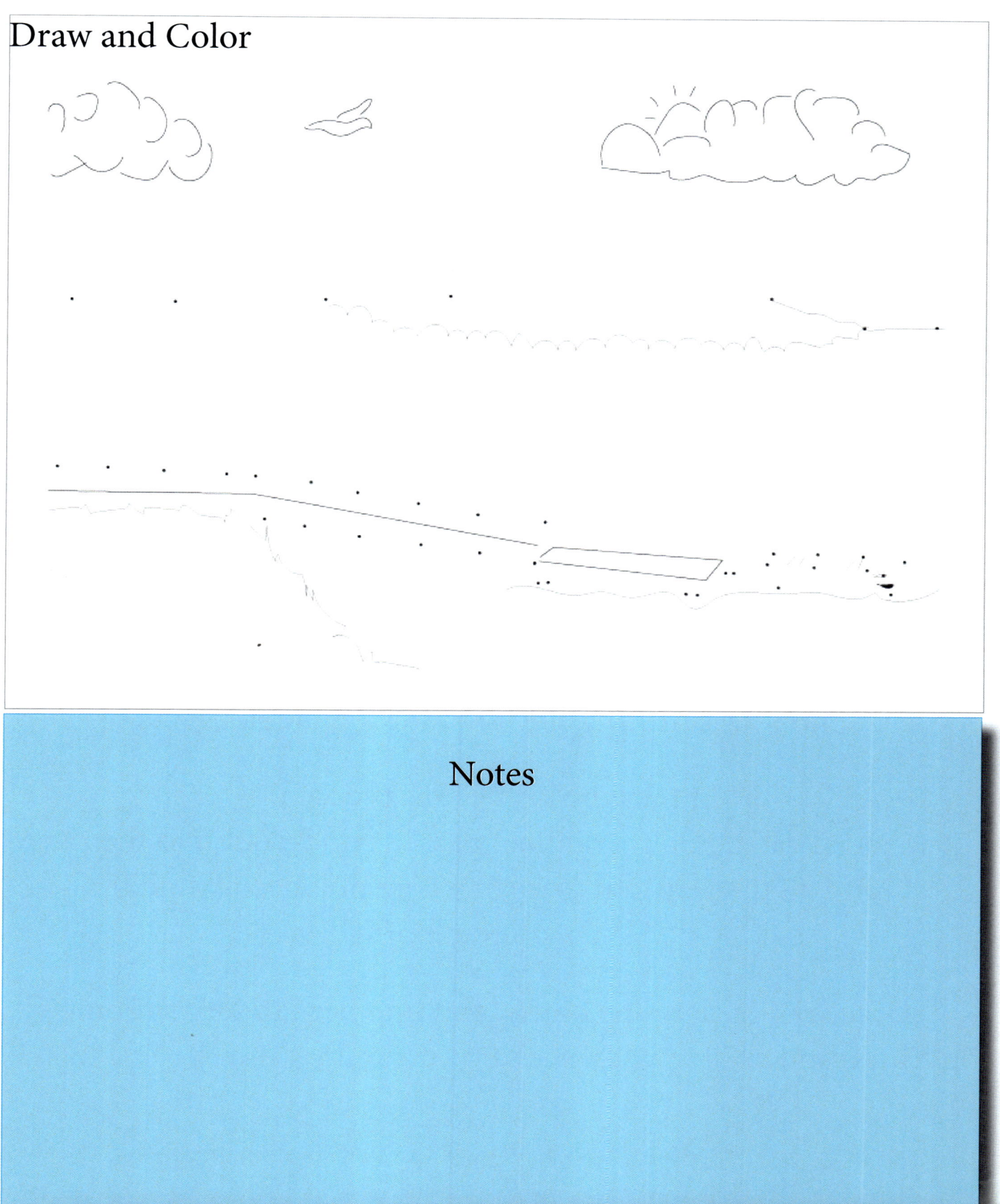

Notes

There was no one in it,
and it was drifting slowly toward grandpa's dock.

It must be lost, Grace thought.
If we don't catch it, it might float past the dock, out into the river,
and all the way to the ocean where no one will find it.
I must do something!!

Grace ran back to the house, and into her grandpa's room.
In a loud and excited voice she said: "Grandpa, grandpa, wake up!!
There's a boat near our dock, and it's empty.
We need to go and catch it!!"

Grandpa rubbed his eyes and sat up in bed.
Grandma opened her eyes too.

Draw and Color

Notes

Grandpa quickly pulled on his shirt, pants and shoes
and ran to the dock with Grace.

Grandpa lay on his stomach and reached as far as he could.
He grabbed the side of the little red boat as she was floating by,
and pulled her to the dock.

"This boat looks as if she is lost. She's full of water.
No one has bailed[1] her out for days — and look, her rope is broken.
I wonder whose boat she is?" grandpa said.

"She's mine, she's mine," shouted Grace.
"She came here all by herself to be with me.
I'll take care of her. She's mine!!"

Draw and Color

Notes

The little red boat smiled.
She was so happy to be rescued, and even happier
when she heard Grace say, "She's mine."

A new home would be so nice,
with Grace to love and care for her.

Then grandpa said, "Grace, the little red boat
must belong to someone. The storm must have broken her rope
and the wind and tide[1] brought her here.
She is not our boat. We must find her owner and give her back."

Grandpa pulled the little red boat up on the shore.
He turned her on her side so all the water ran out,
and the little red boat felt much better.

[1] tide: The rise and fall of water in an ocean and in the rivers and streams that flow into the ocean, that occurs about once every 12 hours. The tide causes a current that will move a boat floating in the water.

Draw and Color

Notes

Grandpa tied her to the dock,
and carefully looked for the owner's name.
But there was no name.

Over the next few days, grandpa called people
on the telephone trying to find the owner — but
no one was missing a little red boat.

Grace asked grandpa to help her take care of the little red boat.
They washed the inside and outside, until she was clean,
and grandpa borrowed some oars from a friend.

They had fun in the little red boat.
Sometimes they rowed her across the cove
to the island to pick flowers.
Sometimes they sat in her and fished in the cove.

Draw and Color

Notes

Every day when Grace woke up,
she ran to the dock to hug the little red boat
and say, "Good morning!!"

Every evening, after dinner,
as the sun was going down,
Grace ran to the dock to hug the little red boat again,
and say, "Good night!!"

Draw and Color

Notes

One day, the owner of the little red boat called grandpa, and asked to come to grandpa's house to pick up his boat.

Grandpa and Grace met him at the dock.
He looked at the little red boat and said, "Yes, this is my little red boat. The storm must have taken her away."

He noticed how clean the little red boat was, and how nice she looked. Grandpa said that Grace had found the boat, and helped him clean her.
The owner asked Grace if she liked the little red boat.

The little red boat waited anxiously to hear what Grace would say.
If Grace said yes, maybe the owner would let Grace and grandpa keep her.

Draw and Color

Notes

Grace did not say anything to the owner at first. She was hoping the same thing as the little red boat — maybe the owner would let her and grandpa keep the little red boat.

Finally she said, "I really like the little red boat. We have been fishing in her, and we rowed her to the island to pick flowers. She is my friend. I like her very much."

The owner stood very quietly, thinking for a few minutes

Then he said, "I think the little red boat would be very happy here. I don't need her anymore, and it looks like you will take good care of her. Would you like to have the little red boat?"

Grandpa looked at Grace and smiled, and Grace smiled, then she laughed, then she shouted, "Yes!! I would love to have the little red boat. Thank you, thank you!!"
Grace and the little red boat were very happy.

Draw and Color

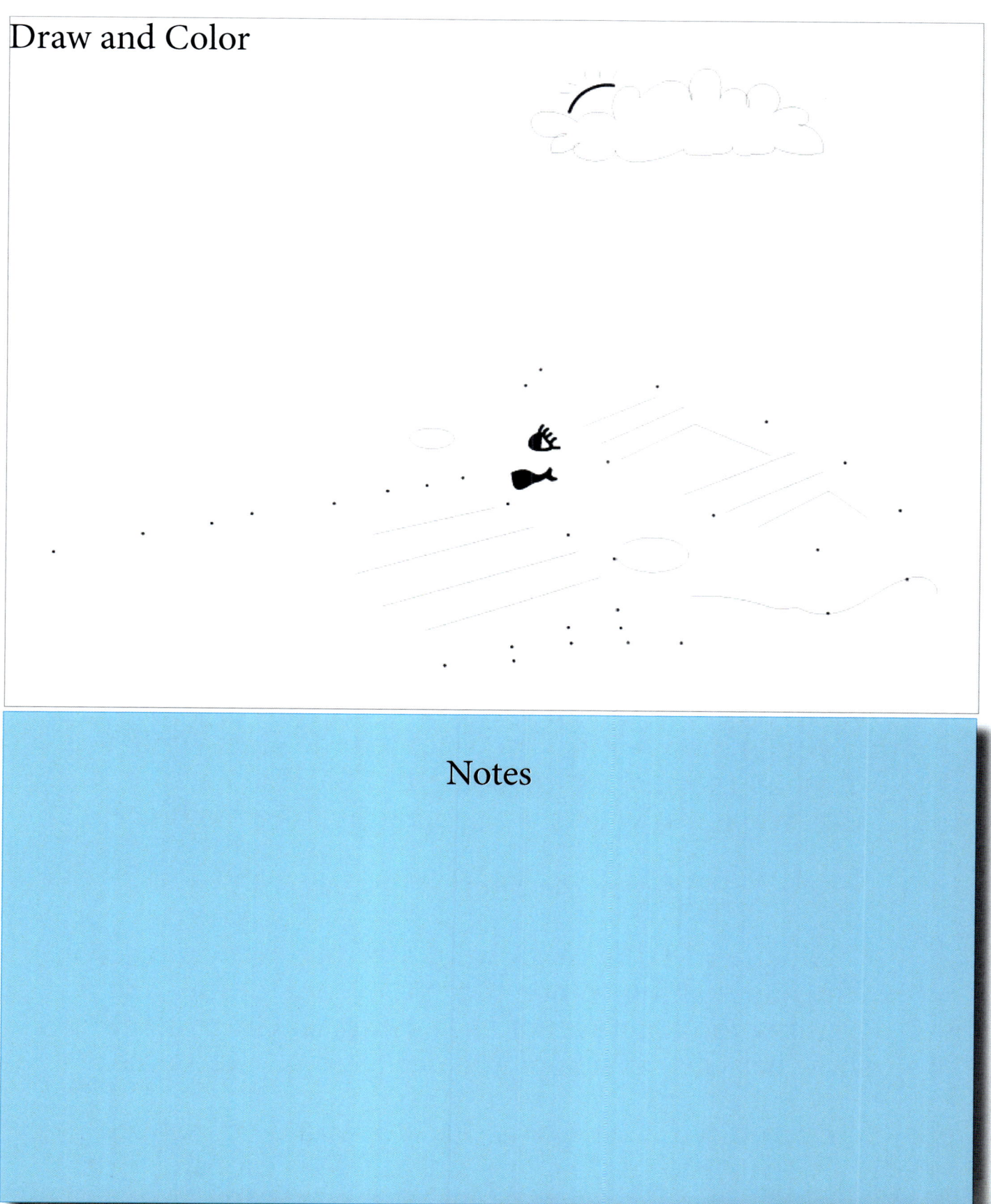

Notes

The next day, Grace and grandpa painted the little red boat with a new coat of red paint. They bought new oars[1] and painted them white. They painted the seats white too. And on the back of the boat, they painted a name. Can you guess what they named the little red boat?

They named her *Little Grace*.

Grace and *Little Grace* were together every day, rowing and fishing. When the end of the summer came, grandpa took pictures of *Little Grace* so Grace could show her class at school and her friends back home.

She promised *Little Grace* that she would come back every summer to see her, and she did, for years and years.

---

[1] oars: A long round pole with a broad blade at one end, which is dipped into the water, then pulled or pushed against the water to move or steer a boat.

Draw and Color

LITTLE GRACE

Notes

Each summer, after Grace went home to Worcester,
grandpa and his friends carried *Little Grace* to the barn and left her
there for the winter, sheltered from the snow, sleet and rain.

Little Grace missed Grace, but she was not lonely.
There was a very old boat in the barn
that could not be used anymore.
The very old boat and *Little Grace* became friends
and talked to each other every day.

There were birds nesting in the barn. A raccoon lived there too.
They talked to each other all through the winter.

The little barn was very noisy.
The little red boat was very happy.

Draw and Color

Notes

The years passed, and Grace grew up. She went to high school, then to college, but she still came to Maine to visit grandpa and grandma and the little red boat.

Grandpa and grandma used the little red boat too.

In a few more years, Grace married, and had her own children. She brought them to Maine in the summer and they played with the little red boat. They loved her too, just like Grace did.

Draw and Color

Notes

Listen to this story on StepUp App

Step 1

Scan this QR code 1 to download StepUp App

Step 2

Open 'Scan and Learn' in the StepUp App and scan QR code 2.

Listen to the audio version of "The Journey of the Little Red Boat" story.

Readability and Related Details

Rating	A
Category	Fiction
Words	2166
Unique words	469
Sentences	181
Reading Time	15-20 minutes
Grade	K - 3

Exercises

1. What is the main plot of the story?

2. Who are the main characters of the story?

   Ⓐ Grace and her grandfather
   Ⓑ The little red boat
   Ⓒ Grace, The Little red boat, Grace's grandfather and grandmother
   Ⓓ None of the above

3. What is the initial setting of the story?

   Ⓐ A house on an island on in a river in Maine
   Ⓑ On a farm in Maine
   Ⓒ On a boat
   Ⓓ None of the above

4. What is the time setting of this story?

   Ⓐ Summer
   Ⓑ Winter
   Ⓒ Autumn
   Ⓓ Rainy Season

5. Write the plot of the first part of the story "The Journey of the Little red boat". Write in your own words.

6. Explain the character of Grace and her emotions in the story "The Journey of the Little Red Boat".

7. Include in the story at least one example of a marine life creature that would inhabit a tidal river in Maine,
    and explain how you were able to determine that this creature would live there.

8. Which character or characters would tell the story and why did you choose them?

9. What title and subtitle (a subtitle is a short phrase that adds more detail to the actual title) would you give the
    story?

10. How do the pictures and illustrations help in understanding the story?

Answer Key and Detailed Explanation

Question No.	Answer Key	Detailed Explanation
1		Looking at the story idea for "The Journey of the Little Red Boat," we can see that the plot (main story) is focused on the little red boat. All of the events that take place and all of the actions by the characters and the location (setting) are caused by or directed at the little red boat.
2	C	Looking at the story idea for "The Journey of the Little Red Boat," we see four characters: a young girl named Grace, her grandmother and grandfather and the little red boat (remember that characters do not have to be human or even real).
3	A	Looking at the story idea for "The Journey of the Little Red Boat," we can see that the initial setting is a house on an island in a river in Maine.
4	A	The time setting is Summer.
5		While sitting on the deck, Grace and her grandfather see an empty red boat drifting into view on the river.
6		The author describes Grace's emotions in several situations: excited (when she sees the boat; when grandpa catches it; when the owner gives the boat to Grace and grandpa); affectionate (she hugs the boat each morning and evening; she visits the boat each summer for years); anxious (when she is waiting for the owner's decision on what to do with the boat); happy (when she and grandpa use the boat to go fishing or pick flowers.
7		Answer may vary
8		Answer may vary
9		Answer may vary
10		With graphics, we mean photos and illustrations. Graphics can make a story more interesting, and they add length to a story. By including illustrations in this story, the author almost doubled the length of the story. In a picture book, photographs and illustrations are often used to help describe the setting because then the author does not have to provide as much written detail; the reader can look at the photos and illustrations and learn many details that way (for example, how a character looks or is dressed; what a building or scenic view or street looks like)

How Author's Develop Story Ideas

Author Smith's Steps to Growing Your Story from the Story Idea

Step 1 ▶ Plots

The story idea appears to have only one plot (main story line) and it is all about the boat: the boat drifts to where Grace and her grandparents live, they rescue it, tie it to the public dock and post a Boat Found sign as they leave for home. The plot focuses its words and pictures on the boat; neither Grace nor her grandparents are mentioned or shown in pictures in the first 23 pages.

But then on page 24 the author introduces a subplot. The subplot focuses its words and pictures on Grace and her grandparents through page 27. Then the plot and subplot come together and become one on page 28, when Grace looks out the window early in the morning and sees the boat floating in the water near grandpa's dock. From this point on, the author talks about the boat and Grace and her grandparents.

Mr. Smith also grows his story by adding events to the plot. For example:

- A description of the little red boat's life at its original home, mentioning how it gets towed behind the sailboat when the family takes a sailing trip, and what things it sees from its dock.
- The rainstorm that fills the boat partly with water and breaks its tie line, and the start of its journey downriver as a result.
- Details of the boat's journey downriver – its encounters with a rock, sailboats, seal and cormorant birds.
- How grandpa and Grace clean the boat, use it, meet the owner when he comes to claim it, paint it and add a name to the stern (back) of the boat after the owner gives them the boat.

- How Grace at first and later on with her family come to visit the little red boat and grandma and grandpa each summer, for years.

The author also adds plot twists. A plot twist is an unexpected event that takes place in a plot. The plot twists in this story are: when the family sells the sailboat; when the storm breaks the tie line; when the boat is rejected by the things she meets on her journey downriver; when she is rescued by Grace and grandpa; when the owner gives the boat to Grace and grandpa.

Step 2 ▶ Characters

We mentioned earlier that there are four characters mentioned in the Story Idea. The author grows the story through the characters in many ways.

1. Grandpa is included in many events: running to the dock with Grace and grabbing the boat, emptying the water out, tying the boat to the dock and looking for the owner's name; calling people to find the boat's owner; helping Grace clean the boat and joining her in the boat to fish and pick flowers for grandma; answering the phone when the owner calls and inviting him to come and get his boat; going to the dock with Grace to meet the owner; helping Grace paint the boat when the owner gives it to them; storing the boat in the barn for the winter.

2. The author tells the reader why Grace is at her grandparents' house, and what she enjoys doing when she is there.

3. The author describes Grace's emotions in several situations: excited (when she sees the boat; when grandpa catches it; when the owner gives the boat to Grace and grandpa); affectionate (she hugs the boat each morning and evening; she visits the boat each summer for years); anxious (when she is waiting for the owner's decision on what to do with the boat); happy (when she and grandpa use the boat to go fishing or pick flowers)

4. The author adds other characters to the story: the owner of the boat, the owner's sailboat, a talking rock, talking sailboats, a talking seal, cormorant birds and blue birds, an old boat and a raccoon.

5. The author adds interest and dialogue to the story through a writing technique called "personification." Personification means giving human abilities to something that is not human. In this story, the author gives the little red boat the ability to talk and have feelings He describes the little red boat's emotions in several situations: happy (when she is at her original home and takes trips tied behind the sailboat; when Grace and grandpa rescue her; when the owner gives them the boat; when Grace hugs her; when she is in the barn for the winter and has a boat and other animals to talk with); sad (when the owner sells the sailboat, which is the red boat's best friend; when the rock and sailboats tell her to go away, the seal does not stay with her and the cormorants fly away); scared(when the storm breaks her rope and she drifts down the river and thinks she will drift all the way to the ocean and sink before anyone finds her).

6. The author also gives other characters the ability to talk and have feelings, such as the rock, sailboats, seal, birds, raccoon and an old boat.

7. The author also tells the reader about what the little red boat, Grace and the boat's owner are thinking to themselves and not sharing with the other characters. For example: when the owner comes to claim his boat, both Grace, the boat and the owner have private thoughts that only they and you, the reader, know about. Adding a character's private thoughts adds to the length of the story and makes the reader feel like they are included in the story.

Step 3 — Place Settings

Describing the setting can help the reader understand events in a story, and should complement the plot and personalities and actions of the characters and add to the length of the story. In this story, the author describes the setting as a salt water river in Maine. Typical of salt water rivers is that they have a current (tide), and in this story, the tide moves the boat downstream on its journey. Also, the animals and objects that the boat meets are found in Maine (seals and cormorants, for example). Also, Maine has snow, sleet and rain, which are the reasons that the boat is put in the barn for shelter, a barn where all the inhabitants have conversations.

Step 4 ▸ Time Settings

The time period for this story could be any recent time in which the clothes that Grace, her grandparents and the owner are wearing are typical. Within the story, the author does not tell how old the boat is or how long it was at its original home, or how long it took to complete its journey down the river, or exactly how many year's grandpa and grandma owned the boat and Grace came to visit the boat. These time periods are not important to the story.

The author does mention that while the boat was at her grandparents' house, Grace grew up and went to high school and then college and then had her own family. Also, during the boat's journey downriver, the time changes from daylight to nighttime to daylight again.

Step 5 ▸ Adding Graphics

By graphics we mean photos and illustrations. Graphics can make a story more interesting, and they add length to a story. By including illustrations in this story, the author almost doubled the length of the story.

In a picture book, photographs and illustrations are often used to help describe the setting because then the author does not have to provide as much written detail; the reader can look at the photos and illustrations and learn many details that way (for example, how a character looks or is dressed; what a building or scenic view or street looks like).

Instructional Information

Nonfiction:
1. An empty little red boat drifted into the cove in front of the author's summer home in Maine, and the author grabbed the boat as it passed his dock.
2. The author emptied the water out of the boat and looked for a name or license number but there was no identification.
3. Grace is the author's granddaughter and she comes to Maine to visit.
4. There are rocks, seals, cormorants, sailboats, lobstermen and sightseeing boats on the river where the story takes place.
5. The family likes to play card and board games at the kitchen table after dinner, a tradition that has continued through five generations.

Realistic fiction:
1. Grace could have been there the day the boat drifted into the cover, but she was not.
2. The owner of the boat could have shown up to claim it but he or she did not.
3. The author could have kept the little red boat and he and Grace could have cleaned and painted it and used it to go fishing or pick flowers, but he did not keep it because the family already owned a boat.
4. Grace will grow up, and presumably become formally educated, get married and have children, as described in the story, but for now she is still a little girl.

Fantasy:
1. Boats cannot talk, have feelings or have faces that change to reflect their moods.
2. Rocks, seals, sailboats, raccoons and birds cannot speak or understand English.

Personification: The little red boat, sailboats, rocks, seals and birds have been given some human capabilities.

Two Level Story: At several places in the story, the narrator addresses the reader directly by asking questions. Otherwise, the narrator tells the story without interaction with the reader.

Made in the USA
Middletown, DE
30 May 2020